BOOM! AND ADVERSITY

DR. JOHN D EMENS

John D. Emens

Copyright © 2018 John D. Emens

ISBN: 978-1-7323147-0-2

Dedication

For my wife Janie

--Special thanks to Michael L. Schurch for his help in the production process of this book.

Introduction

Anatomy of an Ordeal

In October of 2015 I had an accident and fell, shattering my right ankle with a triple compound fracture. The local hospital operated, placing metal plates and screws in the damaged area. Unfortunately, during post-op I slipped into a coma which lasted four weeks in which I was completely unresponsive. It was a last ditch procedure that was performed using a strobe light, which roused me from my "sleep;" when I awoke, I had amnesia—I recognized no one except my wife. Weeks later I was released from the hospital; she took me home, and as an able caregiver, began to nurse me back to health. By Christmas of 2015 my long-term memory began to come back, and I was able to recognize my family members as we celebrated Yuletide festivities—all of us felt richly blessed at my remarkable recovery.

I seemed to be making good progress, and by January of 2016 I was up on a walker and using an exercise bicycle at home. Yet, in April the screws started coming out of the ankle, which was massively infected and pushing out the hardware. The local hospital wanted to operate immediately, citing the strong likelihood of amputation. We chose instead to go to Riverside Methodist Hospital in Columbus, Ohio, where multiple doctors from Orthopedic ONE preformed four surgeries in twelve days; they shredded the infected leg, removed dead ankle bone, and placed a tunnel port in my chest in which massively strong antibiotics were placed order to try to save the leg. Overall, the prognosis was not good.

Following the surgeries, doctors wanted to send me to a long-term care facility, but my wife intervened and demanded she take me home. Having been a nurse's aide for fifteen years and a certified phlebotomist, she cared for me night and day, and was taught to flush my tunnel port and dump liquid antibiotics into my chest daily. I was in a horrific wasteland of delirious pain, and given strong opioid painkillers, from fentanyl to Oxycodone, to Percocet for many weeks. By midsummer, the surgical wound started healing, but by now I was "tripping" horribly on the painkillers. I was sent to rehab where I spent over two weeks getting straight. Three weeks after being released from rehab, I had an additional surgery, where they rebuilt my ankle with a bone graft from my shin (with non-narcotic painkillers, mind you). Coming home, we had no idea if the bone graft would take, or if I would ever walk again.

It took another five months for the leg to heal, and during this time I wrote two manuscripts; one a collection of Christian essays, and another of short stories. It was a remarkably hard waiting game seeing if the bone graft would take. In January of 2017 the first X-rays came back. Alleluia! The bone graft had taken and been a success and there was no sign of infection at all. Within a few months I was up walking with little difficulty. We rejoiced wholeheartedly. *Miracles do happen.*

Yet there was now a new complication. I had been a diabetic for twenty years with weak kidneys for years. Now, due to the strong antibiotics used to save the leg, my renal function was further compromised. By summer of 2017, I was in stage-five kidney failure. I then went to The Ohio State University Wexner Center in Columbus, Ohio to be evaluated for a kidney transplant. I hoped and prayed for a living kidney donor, and a second chance at life.

But the story does not end there. In November of 2017 I began to have small wound issues again with the ankle. This continued into 2018, where in June, an MRI was done which showed that infection had come back into the ankle. In July an exploratory surgery was done, and the cultures showed that the infection had indeed returned and was now in the bone. Since there is no way for a kidney transplant with any infection, there was nothing left to be done—the leg had to finally come off.

During this past year I began working on this collection of poetry: "***Boom! & Adversity.***" It is a literary expression of a blessed, thankful man, who has found that struggling through a continued painful, fiery, roller coaster ordeal has only heightened his well-being and sense of purpose. Life for all us is truly a work-in-progress. The succulent struggle of pain, confusion, and moments of deep darkness has only deepened my faith and given me true appreciation for even the smallest blessing of this life. The piercing sweetness of my Lord has prevailed, and His faithfulness continues to be revealed daily.

Where I go from here is anybody's guess. I continue to wait, pray, and live—live with grateful joy and a thankful heart that I can continue to write and spirit the goodness of the Maker in spite of undergoing abject difficulty and suffering. I hope this small collection of ditties find the reader moved, entertained, and touched in a good and meaningful way.

Blessings,

--J.D. Emens
August 2018
Marion, Ohio

Poem	Page #

BOOM!

BOOM!

A toddler falls down and goes
Boom!

Grown-ups scurry and pick him up.
Child cries, mostly scared.
Hugs, kisses, and everything is O.K.

A teenager falls and goes
Boom!
He or she is grounded until they learn better.

An adult falls and goes
Boom!
> Nobody picks him up. Nobody grounds him or her.
> Mostly no one cares. Whilst on the ground in pain,
> onlookers laugh and point.
> Alone, the adult must make a choice—accept circumstances
> and make the best of it, or blame.

I have chosen to make the best of it. I don't understand the how's or whys,
and I don't know where I am going. But I know in my heart, that the only
one to pick me up from this

BOOM!
Is Moi.

--I can't be grounded, because I am already on the ground…

TADPOLE

The tadpole is born without arms or legs.
He doesn't know what or why he is spawned
In the mucky water in the old wash basin
Behind the old filling station.

The water is warm when the sun shines and he starts to mutate. He is scared
And confused. His body is changing and no longer his. He frets and with
sublime angst he observes the deformities take place. He is at his wit's end.

But at his worst is his finest hour. Before the wash basin is overturned and
sold at the yard sale, he jumps out on his new, fledgling legs to safety.
The tadpole is now a frog, and his odd mutant transformation is no longer
something to be feared…it has been his destiny and his salvation.

It all now makes perfect sense. Happy, the frog now uses his new legs to jump
into the nearby pond only to find hundreds of others like him. They welcome
him and give him his own lily pad.

He lives a long, blessed life, finally knowing exactly Who and what he is. He
croaks with joy along with the multitudes of other froggies.
He has come home. He smiles a wide puckish grin.

He belongs.
    He is thankful.

WELCOME DARK THUNDERHEADS

The thirsty sunburnt itchy blades of grass are moping. No rain. Brave clover is wilting. Yawning Earthworms are parched. Dandy lions aren't.

Relentless August rays turn mushrooms into insipid, baleful, grousing brittle. Lawn mowers are idle. No reason to mow. Swimming pools are glad chock full. Sunscreen sloppily applied liberally ubiquitous. Angry radiators overheat. Lemonade stands rake in the cash. It is hard to stop a Trane.

Dogs and Cats water bowl frenzy. Furtive fowl gaggle water's edge.
Steeds stay barn shadow. Sluggish rainbows hunker down in deep pools of stream bed. Buck, doe, and fawn lick morning leaves dew. Bored mosquitoes fuzz about in deep forest musk. Sturdy queen Ann's lace smile.

Burnished wheat fields golden crisp brown as farmers lament. Weathermen and Native American rain dancers have new importance. Carbon monoxide, ozone depletion and global warming are to blame. Dark clouds on the horizon are an answer to prayer. Thankful, grateful rain falls.

All rejoice! All rejoice!

REJECTION

She didn't know why he didn't kiss her. Maybe this lad didn't smooch on the first date. Maybe she should have worn the shorter skirt. Maybe she talked too much and scared him away. Maybe he was shy. Maybe he didn't like girls at all.

Guess it was a blind date gone bad.

Besides, he was just a farm boy, and plowboys don't make coin.
Yeah…it was a good thing. Better go hunting elsewhere for some greener deep pockets… (What a shame…he did make her smile and he did have a bitchin truck).

JOY & PEACE WITHOUT THE TENNIS RACQUET

The last eighteen months just plain crazy: Six surgeries, the battle with painkillers, and incessant wound care sixteen months either bedridden or in a wheelchair.

--Yet joy and peace have prevailed.

Someone once said, "people are as happy as they want to be". I have chosen to stay happy, in spite of intense hardship, pain, and confusion. The whole process has brought me closer to my devoted wife, and my caring, personal Maker.

I have had the time to think long and hard about many things. I have written two books and compiled a third. I recognize more than anything else, that even though I have been a center of attention, I am not the center of the universe…that role belongs to the One and Only, the one who is, was, and is to come.

When one realizes that they are loved and cared for from Above, when shit breaks out down here, there still is a certain unwavering peace. In such messy times, we can still recognize there is no panic in heaven, nor should there be on earth.

No one ever said that life would be easy, and you know what? Life is not easy. But I know and that I am and will forever be a work-in-progress, whatever that means. I may not walk again, or I may never play golf again or hold a tennis racquet.

Yet, that is okay. At some time in our lives, none of us will hold golf clubs or tennis racquets. We must accept our limitations to liberate our possibilities.

Times change. So, must we.

But if our peace and joy come from the way we look, or what we can or cannot do, then they come not from within. My peace and joy come from knowing a man who was despised and hated two-thousand years ago.

He still loves me just the way I am, even if I am physically not the man I used to be.

In fact, there is a piercing sweetness in knowing the man when nothing else seems to be working. Putting myself completely in His hands has freed me from self-adulation and navel gazing.

I may not be what I want to be, but I may be what He wants me to be. My life is a novel, an unfinished book; I am not the author nor the director of the screenplay. I am only the actor reciting the lines and following the cues as best I can.

Resignation of control only leads to perfect freedom and the chance for my inner being to rejoice for what I am, made for, and what my new stewardships might entail.

Sure, I can question "why" and wonder why sometimes the pieces don't fit neatly together, or I can accept my puzzle is still intact and blessed even though the borders, colors, and arrangement of the pieces have changed.

Like I said, I don't write the script. My job is to trust the lines, and be the best actor I can, come hell or high water. Let opening night decide the efficacy and the proof of the putting.

My job is to pray. His job is to answer. My role is to then accept and obey. By doing so, joy and peace are mine forever. I must always be comfortable in the "skin that I am in," Even though my skin—flesh and bones—are not immutable...for in the final analysis,

Even if my body is broken, it is still sacred...and I know that whatever form or shape I am in, I am still treasured from Above.

PEACOCK BLUES

The male peacock has a fancy plume and many Colors.
The female a dud.

Yet as Pangloss intuited in Candide, "All is as it should be." Some of us are smart, pretty, and have cushy jobs. Others face the daily grind of a life without comeliness or vocational ease.

Yet, it is not ours to ask why. The singer sings, and the painter paints, but the accountant does neither. Yet, all three may be doing precisely their raison d'etre.

The pencil pusher may wish for a better voice, and the singer with good pipes may not be able to balance his or her checkbook, but both may be exactly what they "should be."

Nobody has it all.

We must accept our limitations, to champion our strong suits. to believe otherwise is only to lament the drab, garish colors of the female peacock, whom no doubt never thinks she is not precisely what she was created to be.

"It is what it is," and there is a reason for it. Solid ice never wonders why it can't trickle downstream…neither should we.

SMART CANTALOUPE

Nobody likes green cantaloupe, puckish sour and blithely bitter.
No way to tell a good one 'til cuttin' one open. Gamble at the grocery every
time. Life is like a cantaloupe.

Timing is everything. Marry now, or marry later. Kids now or abort.
Rewarding dream job or self-satisfying moneybags save for the SUV or
borrow loan shark interest.

Rent to own or credit card glamour spanking new 'fridge. Why wait?
Twenty-fist century instant gratification ubiquitous. Microwave blues cause
food tastes like shit but quick & easy.

Kissing on first date a randy standard. Plastic plastic—everything is plastic—
when done, just toss the crap into plastic bag in the plastic rubbish bin.
Convenience rules—go drive thru over set down dinner forevermore.

Nobody talks. Headphones bugger ears and head is stuck in cellphone.
Handwritten notes are dinosaur extinct. Get married in Vegas overnight—
save the divorce papers for next week.

Time is money. Money is time. Neither brings peace. Sit down dinners with
the kids a distant past causes the omnipresent tele trumps family conversation.
Visit grandpa at holiday --god forbid we talk once a fortnight even by phone.

Don't confront issues—just shoot a damn email and be done with it. Go to
church on Sunday c'ept when hungover, which only leaves Christmas and
Easter as a remote possibility.

The cantaloupe grins. Life is ripe as ordained by nature. No road-rage in the
garden. Sweet vintage has meaning. Control freaks panic when cut fruit unripe
and so settle for sloppy cheese-whiz on shabby cracker. --tastes shitty, but has
a shelf life of sixteen years…

Danger is in anything lasting. Love is a four-letter word. Dribble before we
shoot. Check is in the mail. My people will talk to your people. "save it for
marriage!" The priest proclaims as he gives his sermon in a big church to an
aged few. Age-old values are trite and might makes right. All language is
inclusive…god, she truly understands.

SUMMER STORMS IN NORTHERN MICHIGAN

Huddling in the petite living room cottage in Northern
Michigan during late night storm. ambient windows glow bright with every
slashing flashing lightning clips. Cabin wood and foundation creak in
tumultuous wind. Clawing sheets of rain pound rat-ta-tat-tat on shingled roof.
Whipping trees bluster and tempestuous waves crash the beach below. Walls
shudder ubiquitous loud with booming thunder claps.

Candles and flashlights provide the only gleam as we kids joyously huddle
tight.

Power is out.

Gale force winds scream against cottage trembling walls. Dog is under bed.
Parents worry about property damage. We kids giggle and chirp with glee.
God is turning over the apple cart with every exciting boom of thunder. We
marvel shudder like an unrelenting spooky ride at Cedar Point.

We sing camp songs in the dark and break out double stuff Oreos and
lukewarm soda pop. We lay sprawled on blankets and start playing Monopoly
by flashlight. Shit! The lights snap on. Wind quells. Storm has passed. Back to
our bunks way past bed time.

Party over.

LOYAL WIFE

Ankle busted compound three places. First surgery inadequate. Takes five more operations and a tunnel port in my chest for liquid antibiotics to save infected diabetic leg.

Doctors want to send me to the extended care facility. Wife balks. She worked in nursing home for years—she knows the incipient horrors there. Brings me home.

Potty chair. Wheel chair ramp. Hospital bed. First four months changing bed pans and turning my body to evade bed sores. No sleep for the Florence Nightingale.

Pain meds out the ying-yang. Restless sleep my only comfort. Bleary-eyed, I lay in bed and clumsily drink my Ensure and thank the woman whom never forgot her vows...

--Selah

        (Pause and calmly think of that)

CRASH COARSE IN EVOLUTION

We started from the sea. Crawled upon the land. Lost our webbed feet. Became a biped. Hairy and burly we roamed and foraged. Invented the wheel. Domesticated animals Organized into tribes. Became taller as diet improved. Found better ways to organize our societies. Industry and labor saving technical change.

Made cars and planes. Space ships. Using warp technology and traveling through wormholes so intergalactic forays possible.

Become smaller, grey, and hairless. Ears smaller and eyes bulging. Finally crash at a planet far away at a place called Roswell. Denied, lied about, and discouraged from visiting.

Unfriendly third planet from Sol now off limits. No need to share or communicate with them further. Let them blow themselves up as they choose conflict over peace.

Pity…just wanted to be friends…and help them avoid the oncoming black hole. Besides, their poor choices lead them to mass planetary drowning anyway. Silly, myopic, inept, phobic race, they were.

Their loss…many other planets to reach out to…

JUST THE FORGIVEN

(This poem came to me in a dream [for real])

It was late. I rolled over and checked the clock: 11:59 p.m.
I closed my eyes. A moment later awakened by brilliant gleaming white light and I heard loud clap of thunder. I opened my eyes and I was flying in darkness save for surrounding thousands of others also dressed in glistening pure bright white.

I looked back at the blue marble getting smaller and smaller In the distance. I asked the person next to me what that buzzing sound was so clearly audible.

He looked me in the eye and said matter of fact, "Those are the screams."
"The screams?" I said.

"Yes. Those are the screams of those left behind." I looked back and the little blue marble was gone and the buzzing had stopped.
I asked my new friend where we were going. He responded, "We are going to heaven."

"But I can't go to heaven," I said. "I am not perfect." My new friend smiled and said, "Heaven isn't for the perfect, just for the Forgiven."

STRANGERS

She got onto the Trailways bus. Sat down next to a glum lad half her age.
He was reading the sports page. She queried his name.
"Robert, but you can call me Bobby." "Where are you going?" She asked.
"Where is this bus going?" Bobby responded. "Abilene."
"That's where I am going, then."

She looked at him: Jeans and ball cap. T-shirt that said, "Old Navy."
"Don't you care about where you are going?" She softly asked.
"Never thought about it." She shook her head, and said, "Where did you
get on the bus?" "I dunno."

Intrigued and perplexed, she implored, "You must be going
somewhere…" "Looking for my wife." "Where is she?" "With some other
guy." "Then why are you riding this bus?"
He looked her in the eye, and responded dourly, "I got no home now."

"You can't ride this bus forever…" (No response)
"Bobby—you can't ride this bus forever!" He smiled and said, "Lady, you
shure talk a lot."

The bus stopped at a whistle stop diner that said, "Good Food." Bobby
got up and headed for the door to the bus. "Where you going, Bobby?"
He looked back, and said, "To get away from you. My momma always
taught me never to talk to strangers." He gave a weak smile and departed
off the bus.

It was raining. A tear trickled down her face as the bus pulled away.
It wasn't for Bobby. It was for her.

Her husband had just left her, and she was going home to mother.

NO BLAME HERE

We live in an age where no one takes responsibility or accepts blame.
It's always someone else's fault, or a glitch, or maybe lunch was next
Thursday, not today.

Sorry.
It is easier to lie than speak the truth most all the time. Fabrication is simple.
People are so used to inept falsehoods that they mistake sincerity for the
truth. If you say it emphatically with enough hubris and emotion, then it
must be true.

Honesty has become a negotiable term as is morality. There are no rights
and wrongs, rather, it is just how you play it and what you can get away with.
"No harm; no foul" has become sacred litany.

God watches on and shakes His head. He is the forgotten One. He is true,
honest, and blameless. His last name has become "dammit." We pretend He
isn't there. If God exists, then our darkness and insipid untruthful choices
Will come to light. Naaah! There can't be a Deity.

Besides, God forgives everything, so what's the big whoop? The scriptures
say "Vengeance is His." But most people think He is a milquetoast
curmudgeon. God is sweet, kind, and all-loving.
He understands we have to live falsehoods.

But what if we are wrong? What if God counts our sin against us?
What a lousy Creator we must have…better choose a different church or a
more palatably diocese.

There has to be a clergy somewhere who sees it my way.
--besides, He made us…it is His fault if we screw up! You know…there is
no such thing as computer error.

(Think about it).

TO BE PITIED…

I weep at night sometimes. Not for myself, but for the less fortunate:
--The children dying of cancer.
--The young girl who chooses abortion to meet her parent's wishes.
--The old or infirmed who can't afford their prescriptions.
--The successful people with pasty smile void of true feelings, empty or simply dead inside.
--The divorces of convenience that leaves pure, unadulterated emotional wreckage.
--Teachers that don't, and young hopes and minds wasted.
--Mother earth being raped and pillaged for almighty dollar.

They say count your blessings. This assumes you are blessed enough to be able to count. Now we have machines that count and tabulate for us. We live in a digital age, and virtual reality matters more than the actual.

People are things. Expendable. And nothing is perfect or true.

Here is some truth:
 last month a man was shot to death over a cheeseburger. (Must have been some cheeseburger).

--Selah

BARN SWALLOW

The barn swallow is fortunate. It chirps and flits unabashedly off branch and tree limb. God feeds it and it has no ill feelings toward no one.

Perfectly crafted from Above, the swallow is thankful, just for being the drab, silly, tiny creature not worth shooting or making a trophy. Has no enemies.

Simply is.

Lives in the moment and then expires with no remorse.
    (That we could be so fortunate)

THE STREAM WAS BOTHERED

The Stream was bothered. Nobody visited it anymore. Video games reign supreme. Water now comes in plastic bottles. Fish that used to frolic within and were caught by laughing children have now gone the way of the dinosaurs… nobody takes the time to bait the hook on picnic by the river's edge.

The stream remembered the old days where giddy kids did cannonballs into the watering hole and brave, fearless canoes shot the rapids. Horses drank deeply, and campfire songs were the norm.

No use lamenting.

Water now comes from the city reservoir. For each our time must come. But change is hard…it is hard to compete with the Powerball lottery. Usefulness is a thing of days gone by…

Yeah, the stream is bothered, but it still smiles on frosty, sunlit morns.

IMPETUOUS IRIS

Iris, standing tall like sentries, haughty proud, knowing she is far prettier and fetching than any other bloom in this itchy, uncomfortable, jealous, petty grove of squabbling flowers.

The rich textured fabric of her lavender plumes makes the rival blooms packed in full tilt envious. Grows in bunches for there is safety in numbers.

Her purple moist tongues hanging out insolent in the morning sun. Churlish, unhappy at dusk, where no one can kiss her flavor of brilliant color imbued so indeed.

SCRAPPY SEAGULL

The scrappy seagull snitch forages for fish heads before others get there first. Amidst dry, grey Petoskey stone lay dead feathers yellowed by the angry morning sun. Beach smells of perished poison, laying faded bleached bones exposed to azure wash of calming waves lapping shoreline.

Breeze blows fallow soft and canine hoof prints dot the bleached sandy shore. Old grainy parched logs of fire remain from night before. Couple of coals remembering warm.

I, alone on lakes cape smile. This is my Sunday school—in midst of misty orange sunrise on blanket warm August morn. Crack open a cold Budweiser tallboy, and let calm, soft world sink in remarkable.

THE PERMIT

Sleek, spindly flat burnished pancake gleam. Angry when food scarce.
Forages in flats for spongy crab at spiky coral bottom sea. Laughs at fishermen
with pole on flattop boats scanning under surface with polaroid sunglasses to
snatch off glare to find me.

Travel not in schools. Safety in singularity. Too mean to fear other fishes.
Reign supreme for my genus. Smile as rove about 'til dusk when sleep
with rogue blustery gills barely, quiver.

PROUD OUTCROPPING

Proud granite outcropping frocked with spongy green moss beneath overhang. Hardened by millennium aging yet sporting contemptuous lichen bragging strong amidst bleached surface rock escarpment.

Overhead tiny hawks spiral free as a drivel drop of water cascading on percolating brook below. Weeping willow with sanguine sallow limbs weave and wave in light morning breeze blithe. Half mud-clad toads burp soft Morse code bleating at algae donned pond a stone's throw away.

Me? I am munching on Carr table wafers and smushy brie avec crisp chardonnay iced from cooler night before. Light airy Mozart pipes spritely soft from Sanyo boombox on picnic blanket reside. Nothing like weekend vacay in crusty Colorado craggy foothills which obviate spreadsheets joyfully out of irate cellphone range.

Tax season angst is over. Lonesome time to live again lively. Dawn doves coo fear not afraid. Me neither…bragging bonus paycheck direct deposit come Monday. Hungry corner office looming proud.

PRECIPICE

I took my favorite rock to the precipice overlooking the limestone quarry below. Simple rock, pebble really, cleaved asunder grainy mauve center. Shiny from forever jangling in pocket rub loose coins and clunky keychain.

Took pebble from beach in Long Island Sound. Vacay from last year with Susan. Beautiful Susie, long flaxen hair and eyes spaced wide like Jackie Onassis. Broad shoulders and languid thighs. Ivy League and all that. She knew how to make me laugh. She is gone now. Forgot to use turn signal on the Interstate.

Can't keep the Susan pebble.

Toss it into the abyss of my scarred heart and plummet shaft into broken soul of water below. Ripples die out from deep varicose blue surface below. Can see myself in serene reflection below. Empty sallow face gaunt from weeping. Sunken eyes but hold memories dear.

The way she would toss her hair back and sway around with an impish smile and a titter giggle. The way she ribbed me for choosing Urology—said I had a wretched fetish for underskirt female blues and requisite need for sticky rubber gloves.

I never knew why she had to go on the Interstate that day.
--she always said it was quicker than cutting through the village. It was raining, and the semi driver was two weeks from retirement.

Squad car came to the condo. They silent cried too inwardly and shared the sullen sudden ghastly news. They gave me her cellphone—sometimes I look at her selfies from the gym…that silly upturned puckish grin as she flexed grandee for the stupid mega pixels….

I have thrown away the pebble. Will keep the cellphone—can't give up the selfies or shrill goofy voicemail recording…her sepulcher joyous tones from oblivion yesterday. Yeah, dammit.

Gotta keep that God-awful phone.

EMPTY GLASS

Never really wanted to be a CEO. Yeah, the coin was good. Limos sweet and I always had been a cute suit boy. Mom and Dad proud, their boy Head of Fortune 500 conglomerate. Bought them a cottage on Jersey Shore with a lift for the stairs since Papa's Parkinson chewed his legs silly. Always wanted to coach track, maybe at a small college or junior prep. Mediocre athlete was I but knew more than my talent would take me. Loved to watch brimming smile when lad or young lady made a lifetime best. Chose the money trail. Wife left me. Kids hate me. Think I'll have a tummy tuck and look for European Singles online. Them broads dig big coin…they might appreciate what I don't in myself.

Hate mirrors. My eyes are sandy and yellow from squinting "P & L" quarterly reports in the wee hours or feverishly memorized before bloody board meetings. Thank God for dry Tanqueray and late-night dim sum from Chink town.

Never did lines…that's what took Gina from me. Always said she could have the dust if she couldn't have me. Need a dog. Maybe a small one that won't shit everywhere. Chicks dig dogs…would make me seem genuine. Remember Tottie from when I was a kid, Goddamn dog followed me everywhere…made me feel special. Yeah. Special. Needed.

Now nobody needs me, c'ept investors from the other end of my pencil driven vacant mind and a soggy broken heart that feels like thin tinkled ice in an empty glass tumbler. Sometimes I hold up the glass and rub my tongue on the ridges just to feel for a rough spot, hoping to find myself in the process.

Then, laughing inwardly I know I am the glass, shoddy shard of a hollow vessel, emptied into a sallow sea of lonely embers of a fire long burnt out from childhood days of playground kickball and who's on first.

Time to straighten the tie and play king for another day. Job first. Me later.

THE UGLY ARACHNID

Everybody hates spiders, c'ept spiders, who think they are beautiful. Some spindly hairy or goosey slick with legs rubbed fine. Small eyes, yes, and even tiny nostrils unkempt unaware, but for odor seeping struggling bugs making for tasty midnight repasts.

Webs that make Van Gogh envy and spittle drips down single strand into new lair to spawn children of a lesser God.

GOD, I REMEMBER

God, I remember the blessed cigarettes. Mostly Camel Lights but sometimes Viceroys. Throaty gravel in the morn with steamy mug of java. Always could pick me up when low, or calm me down when jittered on bad day.

Or effervescent buzzing bubbles of Miller Lites settling in gut and mollifying evenings après the daily grind. A good 12-pack down shiver off the edge of chock world of cellphone beep and bloody ringtone chirps' nasty.

"Eat light—buzz right!" was college motto, or perhaps no food at all empty tummy garish garner of lubricous barley-pop nirvana. Or trashy munchies a la 3 a.m. just to sate devil hunger-famished alcohol belly. Dim spotty vision before blackout quells with foot on floor to abate bastard bed spins.

High carb cholestafests were best to pull back drink-laden dizzy mind before keys went in ignition homebound thru dangerous cop land. Now, old man. Health first. No smokes, drink, or shit food. Feel better, but shure miss the feckless frolic frivolous fun.

Reckless youth sludges grand memories within the glaring burn of brain cells deficit.

REINDEER SLAY

Unsatisfied Rudolf never played reindeer games…so he grabbed a shiny revolver and killed off large modicum of Santa's deer.

Renegade Rudolf was found hiding out on the elusive Island of Misfit Toys, placed in rugged rusty irons with duct-taped schnauz. The Jury convicted the marauding deer slayer to life in solitary.

Rudy laughed raucous at the sentencing—emphatic that he could raise some serious bucks for an appeal. Besides, Rudolf smartly knew he was the only bona fide venison engine alpha to drive Santa's Christmas wheels. Toys for tots and adults in new cars, are far more important than a bambi behind bars. Nothing matters more than a fast car or a warm cozy cardigan, with the possible exception of a Santa Clause pardon.

THE STEAMY AUGUST TORPOR

The lanky rusty-brown totem post wrangling power lines taut
Split simmering orange evening sky asunder.
Humming crickets drum out percussion for background vocals of
Randy Travis pumping out sweet from old Zenith upstairs.
Trim crusty words from inside.
Pa don't want Ryan to join the Army.
Momma's crying sompin' awful.

I slowly pick an itchy scab on my right bare knee cap.
It starts to bleed. I taste the blood—rich, salty, warm, and a bit gamey.
I pull a dark green magnolia leaf of a branch overhanging our
ratty front porch.

The leaf is damp and dank in the steamy August torpor—I set
It on my oozing boo-boo. It feels cool and soothing.
I release the leaf; it sticks to my knee like thick cold maple syrup.

A wan smile flickers across the corners of my mouth.
I notice it is awful still now…no more shouting.
That means a decision has been made.
That ol' Army ain't gonna be getting' any bigger.

Me? When I grow up I want a steady factory job. Maybe
Make me some good muhlah and buy me a fast car.
Yeah. Get me as shiny bitchin' fast car.

Be somebody.

DIFFERENT CURRENCIES

The glance of love inhabits many forms,
and comes much in different currencies.

Love is not sought for, nor fought for,
Rather, it is given and received.
The shape, size, or years do not matter.
What rubs true important is esprit or Geist,

Glancing clean pure from the eyes, which are
said mirrors of the soul.
Physical attraction is fleeting, and cash balances folly—nothing could be
farther from the truth.

Yet every refractive cell of our inner child
Rejoices frolic with an unwrapped new special friend.
The past is past, and the new is choice tasty fine.

We must cherish each other, as a fragile lily,
Or a sensitive orchid, for only love holds tight which holds at all.
Intoxicating amour absconds one's breath away pronto.
In the end, we love by mutual consent,

Not from need, but by offer pure.
Not from receiving the kiss, but by the gushing water emote slurring the moist
embrace in the very first place.

WE-LIKE FLOWERS...

We, like flowers
don't know we are
sweet beautiful, but We are.
Rain droplets are perfect—each one—without trying to be.

By genuine striving, or insipid duplicity,
we humans silly attempt to be better somehow.
Yet, like the flower and the raindrops,
 each one of us is perfectly crafted by God,
And we can see this, know this, and feel this,

If we can learn to accept ourselves or unlearn how not to.

WINTERS WILL NEVER BE THE SAME

The flighty candle whispers flutters in the itchy wind.

Someone has opened a window. It is a dark night.
The sour harvest moon is hiding behind dim pasty clouds.
Capricious wind kisses the metal shutters.

God, I hate mobile homes—even double-wide's
like this one. They feel like, well like
aluminum foil of a Double Mint Gum wrapper;
It serves its purpose, but for only so long.

When Jimmy died everything changed.
Dad turned to vodka, and Momma's takin' sumpin'
for her serotonin---whatever that is.

Sasha just combs her hair and plays video games
twenty-four seven bigtime.

I've been held back a year again. School says I can't concentrate enuf and
I'm a daydreamer. Mom won't let 'em give me them thinkin' pills they
give other students—says they're of the devil. Makes you do suicide.

When I was a kid I dreamed of being a fireman. Jimmy and I would play
Fire chief in the old Newman place back behind Smiley's pond.

Now I feel like I'm burnin' on the inside. My gut tells me where to go
nowhere all the time. I don't shower no more. I just sit on the front stoop
and think about Jimmy—they say it wasn't my fault, but I knew I could've
saved him.

All I do is dream of thin ice and his screaming cries for help.

Winters will never be the same.
                    Nothin' will ever be the same.

GUILTY AS SIN

We born-again Christians are guilty as sin, --guilty as charged.
We think our faith monopoly pure, armed with the God given right to judge
the oft forsaken world of the weak, the gay, or the uncircumcised, who
we say perturbed are much living a lie.

We want cookie cutter people in a cookie cutter world,
where blue wears boy, and pink wears girl.
And the only true mirth, is the Disney flick fun, where
Shameless smug heroes ride infant pure into the setting sun.

But the world isn't perfect, nor are we.
Only by love and trust can we come to see,
that maybe our problems aren't with "those" or "them,"
but start with us, when we condemn.

Maybe the world isn't so bad at all,
when we welcome those who we claim creep and crawl.
God came to offer hope and rest for all,
not play umpire and make the calls.

The Lord true much and pure of light and life,
not of fingers with accusatory knife.
So, we must embrace hewn much the rough & tumble,
or face a Maker who toward us shouts with angry grumble.

SALARY MAN

They had simple first date.
They kissed at the door.
She invited him in and
offered him a slug or two of Chivas.

They moved quickly to the sofa.
She took off her pullover.
All that was left was a paper-thin tank top.
His eyes bulged like hardened poached eggs.
She cozied up close and began to stroke his forehead.

He felt silly, childlike.
He had never been kissed by a woman before.
She unzipped his fly. He felt warm all over.
She moved on him like an unrepentant serpent on a dead chickadee.

He felt feelings frocked rubbed much like never before.
This indeed was the girl he would bring home to mother.
He wondered how much his salary could afford.

When she finished with him she became coy.
He thought she was playing a game.
In truth, she could not remember his name.
So much for marriage, Hedda Gabler...

AND SO, WE LIVE

Sometimes we look at the face 'cross the table
And all we see is unadulterated pure beauty simple sure.
Eyes, Mouth, and simple impish grin turned up puckish sly gorgeous tasty.

You see a nascent child holding up greasy toad.
So proud she pipes up, "Look Dad, it is watering the lawn!"
Papa shakes head proud and smiles in rejoinder.

Dogs roll over on the sofa and softy croon sweet
Canine rhetoric of joy as you pat their tum tums profusely.
When you stop rubbing, they balk resistant, as if stroking them is as good
for you as it was for them.

Old peoples sit and watch porch-side traffic pass.
Query them about life and truth, and they give monosyllabic answers.
Yet there is great wisdom in their parsimony.
For them, your life is a requisite re-run, they are just there for the credits.

A young man falls down on one knee.
Elated, she chirps,"Yes!"
Both are much fools, but fools beat the odds every day.

The infant shrieks thwapped cleanly from the birth canal. He thinks he is
making a grand miscue, trading the pre-natal penthouse to the nipple.

Little does he know about his life ahead of low-fat, low-sodium, and low
cholesterol eats. --that and late nights with Stephen Colbert.

She lies in bed with her heart failing and blood pressure falling right quick.
Color is draining from her wrought wrinkled skin. Family is there true.
In her last breath, she asks about the soy prices.
Her son fibs and tells her they are goin' up.

She gently smiles and passed on painlessly like soft moonbeams through a
smudged, empty water glass. And so, we live...

John D. Emens

THE Llama

The llama wondered when it would rain. Dry leaves were getting old.
She lifts her head plodding sure, and her calves follow true as they clumsily
ford a small chatty brook.

She longed for her mate, who left her when the calves were born. He was
protection. He brought food. She enjoyed the smattered sunset falling
recluse behind the steep, craggy hills—it reminded her of playing in the
bright deserts as a young kid.

She led her straggling little ones halfway up a hill to a little cave filled with
tasty butterfly copses. It was warm as her calves grovel up against her chest
close. She was content.

The gentle wind whistled mildly. The moon beamed proudly tang succulent
sweet. Canvas of mushy stars framed the soft night sky. Not a cloud
obscuring.

HE SMILED, SHE SMILED

He smiled; she smiled
He nursed his whiskey.
She drank her gin, extra dry.

He smiled.
She smiled.

She scooched closer.
He was lonely.

She an intellectual with nary an orgasm.
More drinks.

Their spouses had the same name: Sandy. They both liked Clinton.
He told a soft racial joke. She chirped out incessant laughter whilst
clutching cigarette randy.

They moved to the patio, candlelight only.
More drinks. His hand now on her knee.
Her blouse unfurled a tad sweet bit.

Their cheeks rubbed alcohol crimson. He loosened tie.
Held hands staring into drinks.
(long pause)
"Do you want to go to my room?" He mumbled.

"No... I better be going. This just isn't me. This is for the check.
    Sorry. Bye."

She grabbed her handbag and exited whilst buttoning Her blouse.
He winced managing a weak smile. When she was gone, he placed his head
in his hands and began to weep softly.

It wasn't him either.

PROUD EAGLE

Why so proud, eagle?
Stand offish, aloof, maybe by instinct self-centered so rightly.
Beak curved ivory smooth silly hooked
for snatching prey.
Stern eyes buggered intelligent with moxie raw pure.
Plumes not, feathered for utility.
Bragging wingspan.
Loyal to young, but indifferent to all others.
Sit high nest sentry lookout, almost phobic in height.
Whoosh down grab fledgling *brookies* with landing gear down.
Never lonely, just by lonesome.
Personally, secure in all ways.
No need for friends…content with whom he is.
--that we could be so fortunate.

LEGAL JUNKIE

Pain reminds us we are human,
--frail, mortal, needy-
and communicates when something is wrong,
Broken, exposed, raw, fettered.
Pain humbles us,
Letting us know we all have expiration dates.
Morphine drip to fentanyl spelunking weeks of oxycodone down to
Percocet—these painkillers are boldface liars, only masking ruptured
blighted nerve cells scream raging with scarred addictive
Haze and mindless maze.
Pain meds needed to squelch the ouch,
But they consume us much, and soon own us.

    Slavery legalized.

Like Turkish Delight, the more we take, the more we need.
Like hell, one soul claimed is never enough.
Yeah, numb it up—the hell with tomorrow—we mortgage tomorrow for
immediate fix pronto until the pills own us. frantic until next prescription
fill. Slippery slope…doctors become gods.
Cure worse than the cause. Wounds healed but now true battle begins.

--got to walk away brave and let shit happen…it is the only way out of
private prison.

FIREFLY

Luminescent glow nocturnal sunshine.

Whisper of wings.
   Pulsating ribbons of spotty bright invectives in fields
   of tassel topped rows of faded burnished maize.

Child pops lightning bug in small, glass jar.
   Smiles at grand marvelous catch. Peers unabashedly
   through window of life to see captive glow.

Eyes bounce with raptured joy, only soon
   eclipsed by nagging guilt.

Take lid off and let captive free.

   Bug buzzes out, rejoins legion dancing carousel glow.
   Child beams proud, emancipating a shimmering sea of light
   against still black night.

   Fireflies baseline glow to flanking bright stars in tag-team beauty.

   Only proud plump, buxom moon trumps all giving bleating blessing
   from above...

BLACK EYED SUSAN SWANKS PROUD

The Black-Eyed Susan swanks proud
with lucid crisp frost on soft bright sunlight petals,
and black hole riveted center.

In a gaggle, Susan's outshine bland maize daffodils,
attempting to lift their heads in spritely glee,
only to bow subservient to these sunflower juniors.

Cluster near thick pond's edge, envy of all.
Drab garish verte reeds bow to Susie's superior favor, as do
overwrought black and tan cattails lean sway dank insecure
like towers of Pisa.

Susie's are a dime a dozen, but smirk nice in chartreuse vase, boasting busty
floral bang for the buck. Baby's breath in sidecar fullness taste tandem
beauty firm. Dried and dead, beautiful gorgeous pressed between
dripping pages of sonnets love vanquished never famished or forgotten.

BEATITUDE BEAUTY

The meek shall inherit the earth,
Even though stomped profound much now,
For power rules and might makes many take flight.
Ouch!

Yet, soft beauty trumps triumph over manhandling
Vices any day. Proud vanity succumbs ignominious folly to
Genuine kisses of kindness random. Mighty tower quaking haughty
maelstrom proud, yet, short lived gain eclipse brief morsel gains only.

Lasting love endures to everlasting and everlasting.
Sweet kittens become alley cats, and tender pups become ferocious mutts,
Yet, human's gentility unmasked frolic joy true in perpetuity unending.

Loss now, smarting candy sucker highjacked from blessed child,
But hardened heart not, will provide piercing sweetness forevermore.
Strong sunlight wilts even big-shot shadow towering foliage, so nubile
greenery sprouts glorious blooms below.

Soft, meek, gentle, perennials outlast prissy, seedy, blustery annuals every
time…the wind blows over them, and they are no more.

A LIFE IN A DAY

Coffee percolates aroma strong. Sassy chirps from morning bird's chatter from open window. Newspaper now lays fallow on breakfast table. Kids scuffle about for backpacks to make bus in time. Soiled dishes in sink give burnt scrambled egg odor rhetoric stiff. Parents peek at bus, making sure all is well in the offing, then shuffle out the door toward avocation of opulence requisite.

Kids bang door home first. Video games and Cheetos galore. Parents arrive late, fatigued to the marrow, so order pizza definite of delivery type. Treadmill not useful tonight instead make it a double.

Late nite news comes on. Kids are in bed. Parents sprawled fatty on den sofa sleepy. Check cellphone for tomorrow's weather. Flounder into bedroom, set both alarms. Sniffles…take the Nyquil into deep sawing slumber. No kisses goodnight, to avoid contagion spread.

Alarms bleat smartly.
Dayquil, and the morning java percolates strong anew.

"Déjà vu all over again…"

ANGRY WATERFALL

Why so angry, waterfall? Sluicing cascades of gorgeous liquid froth crash and settle into stream with gentle tippy-toe rocks. Majestic you are, and changing every day and week depending on incipient capricious rainfall…

Frozen February crust on top of rushing, tumbling water below. Spring time at flood stage, ripping torrents pure smack joyous rapid pace.

Summer drought down trickle and lunker trout hide sleepy in deep pools bend river pure. Autumn kisses frosty morns, and steamy mists hover relentless under the eastern morning sky.

The electric company wanted to dam you, big time. Clog up and make big bucks at your expense. State budget cuts saved the day and preserve your reckless omnipotence.

Fear not—save for kayaks and tubers, your soul is free and clear.
Why so angry, waterfall? You survive trim proud, and rule your own
Destiny—the levy gates of your unrankled spirit are open wide blessed sure!

IF PEOPLE WERE DECIDUOUS

If people were deciduous, then all would change colour year 'round. The brighter the shade, The deeper the hue, --all would be cause for celebration, not division.

If people were deciduous, colour patchworks weave mosaic tart beautiful, and all would contribute, pasting dignity and humanity together as in sparkling grains of a morphing desert Kaleidoscope pure.

If people were deciduous, no one would have a monopoly on the right look or the best colour, and nobody would be light or dark only, but have saucy vivid seasons of smack changing glows inherent.

If people were deciduous, change would be our commonality, not separate us, but only cause acceptance, for each of us would only be renting the colour so long...not long enough to claim ownership of preference for dominance sake.

Diversity would be universal, and prejudicial cowardice be only practiced by the renegade outcasts proper.

Don't forget--variety is the spice of life!

CRIMSON TOES

I think at times my life is blessed,
for God forgave when I transgressed.
He never told me why He chose,
to make His stand with crimson toes.
In former days I stood apart,
far from He who made my start.

He took my wrong, and made it pure,
replacing love for missteps sure.
But now I know, and forever keep,
that He is mine from now 'til sleep.

-Selah

"Adversity"

*--and other mild ruminations
of a compromised man.*

DR. JOHN D EMENS

ADVERSITY

ADVERSITY

Even the word smacks of concern and dread. Adversity sneaks up upon us retro slow, or slams into us like an oncoming train.

--bewildered, we flail about screaming for someone to make things copasetic, better. Yet, adversity has two heads—it brings us together, or people go running. True friends stay close, intimate, whilst sunshine soldiers slide away and take their leave.

Adversity elicits the best or worst in us. But as we struggle, we may grow. We learn about ourselves as much as we glean about the ordeal we face. When it is all said and done, we may be for the better, despite the "ouch!"

Patience comes at a price, but it is the ultimate by-product of a protracted challenge. And when we learn to be patient with ourselves, we become more patient, more understanding, with others.

Wait!

 Adversity a good thing?

As it says in the Book of Romans, "All things work good for those who love God and are called according to His purpose." Yes, sometimes silver linings suck, but truth be known, in the long run, we may be better, stronger, and wiser when we come through the fire, the calamity.

Growth hurts, but we become better people when our essence is circumcised, and we are put to the test.

Christ crucified was a bloody, stinking mess, but good came from it— perhaps the same is true with us?

--it takes rain to make rainbows...

Selah!
    (take pause, and calmly think of that!)

THE PROUD

The proud.
The beautiful people.
Good job.
Good health.
--maybe God given good looks.

They look at you haughty, for they scoff at our weaknesses, our
shortcomings, or the simple fact we are imperfect. Yet, pride is a trap,
because it begs trouble, which punctures the balloon of self-
aggrandizement overconfidence, and quells incipient braggadocio.

Trouble, albeit not desired, brings humility, and humility begets truth, and
brings us closer to ourselves—the real inner child without the outer fluff
of accoutrements of cushy job, or shiny cars.

Humility hurts, but it is the inoculation, the antidote to the infection of
pride, which itself makes us at enmity with others, and actually with
ourselves, surprisingly.

Everybody likes piping hot coffee, but when it grows cold, frigid,
It has no true friends—just like us!

BEMUSED

Sometimes I feel sad, no-not sad, or sanguine, but
Bemused.

    --when I think of my life I have to chuckle.

I am not the man I used to be...in many ways,
I am half the man I used to be. yet, in other ways I am stronger,
Better, bolder, and braver for the infirmities I now bear.

My weaknesses are on the exterior now, not on the inside.
Refined by the fire, I am of a higher grade of a metal worth covet and
Without rust.

    --bent, not broken.

I know my limitations, which is important, for by knowing what I am not
I truly know what I am.

True, I am a smudged glass container, but I still have purpose—I can still
hold water...

    --and that will never change.

GODAWFUL RODENT

Nobody likes the Godawful rodent, except rodents, who are precisely
What they are supposed to be—scurrying little trash-mongering
Mongrels.

    --a bother, a disease carrier, and a pest.

Yet, even the rodent has a place.
He is special like no other,
Perfectly crafted by the Maker to scourge the earth of filth and grime
for smaller rodents than himself.

Yes, he be despicable, but it is not his fault he is lower on the
Food chain. You know, we detest the rodent, but there is a rodent in all of
us, mucking about just to survive daily, to make ends meet.

We, in many ways are scavengers too, trying to eke out unfettered meaning
in this vacant, unsure world, which is brutal all in its own. In the end, we
may not like the Godawful rodent, but then again, the rodent may not like
us either...

UNCERTAINTY

Life is uncertain, which is vexing, confounding, unsettling, annoying, and sometimes unnerving. We long for and seek control in a world without control.

We cannot control the weather, traffic, or the actions or behavior of others, no matter how much we try. We even try to control our Maker, to pray enuf' to get what we want and need.

If we get what prayed for, we congratulate ourselves knowing full well we are blessed. When God says "no," we curse Him, and perhaps change churches or double-down on fleeting rationalizations which, in the end, simply add up to nothing.

In truth, we cannot even control ourselves, and that is the real problem. The more we feel out of touch with ourselves, the more we try to compensate in other ways…like suffering others or just plain kicking the dog.

Things never seem to turn out the way we wish. Trapped, we appear confident on the outside, but writhe frail in the inside.

We fear death, our certain expiration date, and we flounder with low-calorie, low-sodium, and low cholesterol eats to stave off the inevitable.

We exercise frantically, despite the fact our bodies are getting soft, thick, and pudgy without our permission. They say we all have an eternal soul, and that we all have eternal life…the question is where we will be spending it?

  --Paradise, purgatory, or worse.

So, we slap on that pasty, irreverent smile, and make the best of it. Even if on the inside we are frightened, unnerved, or doubtful as to how things will turn out—we feign cool confidence, having silly faith that we can punch our way out of that wet paper bag of life…or cheat death for one more day.

We are fooling ourselves…we know it. But life is a death sentence in itself. We struggle by emotional Braille because we have to. We cower inside but laugh outwardly, shouting down the demons of doubt and quiet despair.

Or we have one more shot of Jack or Jägermeister just to forget our problems altogether.

We know the bell tolls for thee, but we think we can outthink, outsmart, or simply rationalize away our impending fate or fates…which will come upon us at a time not of our choosing.

They say, "Let go—Let God." By giving Him control we relinquish our silly, campy attempts to be in charge, and we forfeit worry and angst when we let Him call the shots.

Peace, they say, comes at a price, yet, peace comes when we let the One and only pay that price. Peaceful resignation of the future gives us inward Appreciation of the present.

    --we give up control to gain control, which is
Almost oxymoronic, isn't it?

And losing that umbrella of pride of control over circumstance is the only way to stop the rain of anxiety and consternation in our fitful, uncertain lives. At times in the military they sometimes say, "Failure is not an option," but then again, neither is life or death.

We simply have to let God cut the cards, and wistfully play the hands we are dealt, and smile inwardly on gray rainy days…

COURAGE

Courage is a strange thing, and it takes many forms.

--for some, it is a big thing…facing cancer, loneliness, or a job loss.

For others it is just having the guts to get out of bed. We all face battles, big and small, but each time we conquer, we grow, and learn to take that next step, to a new mountain, higher than the one we just vanquished, until we discover the truth—namely, that the mountain is us, and whether we are ascending or descending we can affect the outcome—just as much as the outcome can affect us.

Amen.

John D. Emens

BEING THANKFUL

Always be thankful!
Praise Him in the heights, and praise Him in the
Depths.
--it's another day, and another
chance to make someone else's life better,
more beautiful, and more meaningful.
Think not of yourself and your woes,

But rather, how you can bring joy & peace to your neighbor
despite what you are going through.
--others lack
--others hurt, and others need.

Beauty is not in receiving, but in offering, giving, and always knowing we
are all in this together.

No man is truly an island.
We must look about and strand no one.
And no matter what—be thankful!

WINDOWS INTO THE FUTURE

Today the windows were crying.
--a gunmetal grey day with showers galore.

Stuck inside, I ponder much. Crazy eighteen months, living
almost entirely in this small house—my sanctuary.

It takes many months for wounds to heal, on the inside as much as the
outside. Yes six major surgeries and a reconstructed leg, but eighteen
months in sanctuary to look at myself,

To see all the silly, wrong, and hurtful things I have done to myself and the
ones I hold dear.

Self-forgiveness is hard. True, life is a daily "do-over." But sometimes
un-doing isn't as easy as it sounds. I want to start over at the age of 56, which
isn't likely.

    --this old body is recalcitrant, stubborn, and old ways die hard.
Reinventing this old wheel will take a lot of work, grace, and blessing.
I may have already used up all my "second chances" and my "Get out of Jail
Free" cards.

Still, there is time left on the game clock. I am still breathing, thinking, and
my heart ticking. I may not walk right, or talk right, I may be beaten, but I
am not defeated.

I hate the term survivor. Overcomer. Yeah. Overcomer—I can live with
that. The problem is, that I am still overcoming.

    --I am not out of the woods yet.

I have come a long, long way, but the work is not finished. I pray the
scriptures come true, namely, that "The glory of the latter house is greater
than the former." Yet, the former wasn't that glorious, truly. And the latter
is yet to be seen and realized.

I despise the term "work-in-progress" or we are all a "journey." I long to be
a destination…a done-deal, but I will have to wait, and see how this all
Plays out. And like Tom Petty croons,

"The waiting is the hardest part."
Arguably, patience hurts. Patience sucks. But as long as I am alive and kicking, God may have just saved the best for last.
I don't know, but hope does spring eternal.

So, I look to the future with hope which trumps the ever-present jaundiced eye, dourly dumping sorrow on the morrow. In the end, I have to giggle inwardly at myself, and realize that I am not nearly as important as I would like to think myself. I am precious in the eyes of the Creator, and it's not what I do that matters, but what I am that counts. Not being half the man I used to be, leaves me little choice but to perhaps live my life out being more a "Mary" than a "Martha," if you will.

But that is okay.

I can still look into the night sky and count the stars, and someday choose to dream of a destiny I might never see, nor ever live, but maybe recognize the role I now play is one I was intended to play all along.

This being the case, I have no choice but to humbly fall on my knees. and accept His will, for only by doing so, can I have Peace…His peace, Now and forever.

Amen.

DEAD CONCH SHELLS

I remember the bright beautiful multi-colored corals whilst scuba diving in Cayman, or the gorgeous conch shells found snorkeling in the serene azure waters off of San Salvador, Bahamas.

We'd dive 20 to 25 feet down and glom onto the live conchs, and bring them back to the ranch, where Minerva would rustle up some tasty conch fritters from her petite kitchen. Live conchs are teeming beautiful, with rusty light brown or mauve pink centers of the shell.

Outside Minerva's kitchen in the backyard were a boneyard of hundreds of dead, empty conch's shells, shucked and harvested for their pink tongues of Succulent meat. The dead shells piled high bleached alabaster dull from the unrelenting Bahamian sun.

Many of us are like those dead conch shells, pretty and spritely colorful on the outside, but sepulcher hollow inside.

We adorn ourselves with magnificent shiny toys, cars, and homes, and brandish lovely and garish frock, to the envy of all. But inside we are empty, insipid, lonely, frazzled, or be leagued.

The world teaches us to brazen shine outwardly, like the just Armor-All dash of our spanking clean motor car. But our engines are vacant, dubious, weak, and shallow. We shadow-box our way through life, not the wiser of Our fragile state of being.

Jesus castigated the Pharisees, with their long rich flowing robes but inside were hollow rotten to the core. We must choose to be people of substance, kind, loving, and respectful of even the most vulnerable, especially ourselves.

We must recognize that inner beauty trumps glitter every time. --To give charity in this way means loving and accepting ourselves first from the get-go, which isn't easy to do. We must unlearn what the world tells us, namely, that vanity smacking proud rues and robs the inner self, even if it feels good at the expense of others.

We must step back, with stern self-appraisal, and choose that harder road less traveled—the one with soft heart and empathetic ways that eclipse the frivolous trivialities of our unkempt, modern world.

By doing so we are born again, the child inside frolicking with joy and inner peace of acceptance of ourselves, which allows us to lick the bawdy varnish off the rough edges of others, and freely see the gorgeousness of their unbounding individual spirit within.

Not to do so imprisons us forever in self-indulgent narcissism and shallow emotional remunerative proclivities. Our outwardly bright conch shells only masque and deride our own chance at meaningful self-love and radical appreciation of the beautiful creatures we are all created to be.

With inner love and healthy self-understanding, we mirror others in the same way…and begin to the enjoy and relish the tasty conch fritters in all of us.

Amen.

LOVE

There are four meanings for "love" in the Greek.
Agape, or unconditional love.
Eros, or passion or eroticism.
Philia, or brotherly love.
Storge, or family love.

Yet to me, love isn't just a feeling, rather it is a state of mind and a
Decision.
--a decision for commitment.
--a decision to stand by someone or something, even when all else seems to
have failed.
--a decision to trust one another despite what seems otherwise.
--a decision to forgo fear of any failure and persevere, regardless of the
consequences.

The scripture says, "love never fails," but sometimes we fail. So we must
remember love is as much forgiving, and understanding when the ones we
love let us down, hurt us, or even wrong us.

Love is a two-way-street, even when it seems to be a dead-end. Paul says
"love keeps no record of wrongs," which is hard to do. Yet, all of us are
imperfect. We make mistakes, and when we can live with our own flaws and
shortcomings, we can accept and understand the lack and the mistakes of
others.

We also learn to accept our own flaws and shortcomings, which only
strengthens us to love more freely in the future. God truly is agape,
unconditional love. No matter what we do, He is there. He teaches us so we
can love like Him, by His example. and the trick is not to balk, or bristle
when things are tough, but to still love Him back.

We live by faith, not be sight. We love by what we are endure, and what
chances we have to make Him proud, and love others even when they don't
love us back. It is a hard row to hoe, but choosing commitment over idle
infatuation or benign, blasé "friendship" proves our worth, and makes us
more like Him.

Love is a daily decision, but it bears eternal fruit.
--Selah.

DEAD MAN WALKING

Kidneys are going bad. Last week's bloodwork confirmed it. A year of massive strong antibiotics to save the leg Have ruined 'em. Doctor says dialysis is months away.

But that is okay, even though it is not okay. We are all one-way tickets, even if some of us last longer than others. It would be easy to curse God for all our early expiration dates, but since each day is a gift, it is unfair to bite the hand that feeds us.

I don't understand why this ordeal has continued, but I am not supposed to. It is my job to pray. His job to answer. My job to obey.

Just because I don't like the answer doesn't mean it is not in His will. He says we are living for His glory, and Psalm 23 says "He leads me in paths of righteousness for His namesake." How we choose to handle the adversity Determines the efficacy of these purification processes.

James says trials and tribulations begets patience. It proves our worth. We must all wait for the eventual "ultimate healing." Train is coming around the bend, for some, sooner than others, and shunning the ride is not my option. So, I play this hand out to completion, fully living each day as if it truly my last.

By accepting His will, I obviate the right to argue, but I gain peace by doing so. The peace that "passeth all understanding;" it reminds me I am on truly on the eternity clock, and time was stopped for me the moment I let Him into my heart.

When the commander says, "Move out!" and He puts you on "the point," You know your days are probably numbered. But He put you there because you are one of His best soldiers, and He needs you to lookout for the rest of the troop.

So, I gladly accept His orders, and the incipient risks involved. I welcome the chance to live for "His namesake," even if I am deep in enemy territory most of the time. I need to bless Him, for he gave me my start in the first place. He chose me, even though I chose Him.

They say, "If He leads you to it—He will see you through it." regardless of the outcome, when the battle is over, I get to come home. and when I do, I want to be carried back on my shield.

For bravery is not negotiable, it has to be earned, proven, and demonstrated lock, stock, and barrel. So, I will walk in His will, and let the "chips fall as they may." Not that I have genuine moxy, but only that I am following in His shoes; he made the ultimate sacrifice, and never complained.

Obedience isn't easy, but no sacrifice is. He did it for the Father, and I do it for Him. They say we all have a "cross to bear." Some crossed are heavier than others, but in the end, they are all lifted off our shoulders, and true life begins.

There is light at the end of the tunnel. It is burning brighter now. So must I.
    -Amen.

BEAUTIFUL DAY

It is a beautiful morning. The sun is out. I can hear the birds tweeting outside my window.

It is May 2017, and I am walking…walking without a boot!
The orthopedic surgeon looked at the X-ray, and called it

"Remarkable."

    I call it blessed.

True, I have to use a walker or a cane right now, but I don't care.
I am upright, and I am walking. The doctors were wrong, and faith was right. Where do I go from here? I don't know about you, but I am going out for breakfast, and I will walk to my car.

Time to celebrate. Time to celebrate! Glory be to the One and Only, for when 'I saw wounded, He saw mended…'

Alleluia!

SO, HE CREATED A DOG...

Dogs are smart. They know us. They know our needs and wants. Sure, they feel our love, but they can tell when we are hurt, frustrated, exasperated, or angry. They assuage ill emotes and quell ad hoc frenetic meltdowns. They bother us with pure, unadulterated charity and make us smile when worlds collide.

They greet us at the door, ebullient wagging tongue, or lick our faces in bed despite bad morning breath. They accept our sour moods and surly vituperations as we bellow at them angst when there is no one else to vent upon. By their stripes we are healed.

Dogs protect us from without, but also from within. Sure, the robber must flee, and the mugger chooses not when we trod at dusk with our loyal bodyguard, but the canine also is a reality check for all personalities coming through our front door. They sense good persons with gentle wag, or whimper growl at undesirables. They are the litmus test for harmless or harmful, and they guard our little ones like a Mama bear with cubs.

They ask little and give much. --God-made little love machines, hooch loyal to the core, and never a complaint unless water bowl hungers too.

Dogs remind us who we are or should be, walking us at night for our needed exercise, or spelling us by soothing licks when wrong mood percolates or anguish spouts.

Our tears are their tears. Fido Prozac rules. We cherish our rescue dogs, but truly dogs rescue us. They save us from ourselves, for we are weak, capricious, moody, mean at times, yet they are quick to forgive, and remind us, at times, to be gentle with ourselves. They talk to us with their eyes and mirror our moods with their body language.

They are a daily antidote, picking us up when we are down, talking us down with a gleeful wag, or horrifying us with humpy leg when the company arrives.

Unabashed instincts of love incisively slice up any bad day, and they instruct us to love others as they love us. The canine golden rule, reminding us that gentleness trumps grumpiness every day of the week. Each pup has a job. To love, protect, and at times, make us feel needed when the world tells us it doesn't.

They trust us, even when at times, we don't trust ourselves, and they give us a daily reality check each time we walk in the front door…bad or good day, waggled chirping body in glee makes all things better for the moment.

At times, the world is going to hell in a handbasket, but have not fear, the dog is here…

True, God is ubiquitous, and all-loving, but sometimes it feels like He isn't there. So, He created dog…

GRAPLFRUIT GLORY

(March, 2018)

With kidneys failing, And the fast-approaching hoof beats of dialysis a certainty, I am little more than a wan, weary, ripe grapefruit, with God gently squeezing the life out of me.

Beleaguered self-surrender is now my raison d'etre, knowing full well my choices are so limited. I may never be cured, but through my hardship I have been healed, made whole, and well-crafted for the shimmering brightness ahead.

As my life fades His glory is revealed….

Yes indeed—a grapefruit glory.

I must become less. He must become more. As the reluctant melting sun grudgingly wisps below the gentle horizon, I choose to be thankful, and purse my lips brimmed open wide to swallow the slow, savory-sweet oncoming warm glow of the eternal sunrise

Awaiting...

Amen.

BAD TO THE BONE

(June 27ᵗʰ 2018)

Today we saw the MRI,
and our hearts sank sick,
the infection is back,
the ankle be clipped.

I was walking good, and driving steady,
but now without leg,
I am passenger ready.

So I must decompress, and recalibrate,
to love Him just as much,
as in times I celebrate.

Crunch-time woes seek one to blame,
but I choose to praise His Holy name.
not that I delight to suffer,
For remorseful incriminations only make things rougher.

So I make lemonade,
when fruit is short,
and trust even more,
when dreams abort.

I seek to find a way
to do His will,
putting down the racquet,
and picking up the quill.

He said, ***"In this life, you will have trouble."***
But I have faith, that blessings will double,
not because I am brave,
but through my wounds, souls might save.

So I push through darkness, in spite of pain,
and thank the Man,
who crucified, took my blame.

Perhaps no more golf, or marathons,

but footprints I may leave,
when I am gone.

He gave His life for those He loved.
I do likewise, without the rub.
I crack a smile, in spite of suffer,
with grand hope, to help the others.

For all need to know,
and must come to see,
that spirit trumps woe,
for all eternity.

I can lose my body, and lament in full,
But nothing can take my everlasting soul.

GOD COMPROMISES THOSE HE LOVES

Truly, God dumps trouble on those he loves,
because he will double their blessings
when they arrive above.

The ones who love,
the ones who trust, God can compromise,
and they won't be lost.

He can count on this—this tethered tight true,
so He makes them an example, full of days perhaps rue.

When He returns, and blessings flow,
He'll reward lavishly the ones
who chose not to go.

It isn't that He loves them any less, au contraire,
He just expects more,
from His very best.

So when we weep & when we cry,
our reward begins the day we die.

This is true as I attest,
for I have suffered
with the numerous rest.

When things go south, and all seems lost,
like Job, we tip out hat, and still thank the boss.

At times like this, we could get angry; we could get mad,
but the crown is golden,
by eschewing sad.

When I die, and life begins,
A life of suffer,
Will turn to win.

No more tears, and no more pain,
"To live is Christ, to die is gain."

Amen.

Eternal Courage

Adversity means opportunity,
if daunting fear is quelled.
in spite of darkness, and ignominious odds,
victory can be secured.

Stay in yourself, head up,
put on that pasty smile.
Grit your teeth,
and move forward despite the impossible.

It doesn't matter what the naysayers utter,
or the pundits pan,
faith & fortitude can prevail.
Win, lose, or draw—take your best shot,
and let the chips fall as they may.

The only failure is in not trying,
weaseling out at the last moment,
or quitting midstream.
press on,
press on,
press on.

In the end, always finish the hand you are dealt,
and crack a smile, knowing full well, that God cut the cards,
and He makes the final play.
You might lose the bet, but He will always provide
your cab fare when you cash in your last chip.

It isn't about winning or losing,
but for obedience sake, letting him do the choosing.
Sometimes he calls us to save the day,
but mostly to fulfill a role to play.

And if we choose to follow His lead,
peace will prevail, and His face will we see.

So take heart, be of stout cheer,
for woe is of the moment, eternity is more dear.

Amen.

Choosing to Lose: *"Defeeted"* but not Beaten

I need a kidney,
but infected leg I've got.
No transplant list for the bloke with the bad wheel.

So i choose to amputate,
horrendous trade-off.
Sure, could do months or years of antibiotics,
but timing trumps first choices,
and infection could always come back.

In sports they say "luck is where preparation meets opportunity."
Then I must be fortunate,
to choose this path,
'cause my chance for longer life,
means slamming the door on natural ambulation.

Times are tuff. I daily live by braille—Faith, believing without
seeing.

I lose a battle to win a war.
I am "defeeted", but not beaten.
I will survive to live another day,
write another poem,
and with sanguine wan smile,
remember…

About *"Boom! & Adversity"* and the Author

J.D. Emens was a college professor and former collegiate All-American athlete who fell and shattered his right ankle. After coming out of a post-op coma, and finding eventual infection in the leg, he went through six additional surgeries trying to save the leg. He was not successful, and after a three-year struggle, had his leg amputated. Furthermore, the strong antibiotics used to try and save the leg compromised and already weak renal function. Emens is now is stage-five kidney failure and seeking a transplant.

"Boom! & Adversity" is a collection of poems exploring Emens' rollercoaster sojourn though pain and suffering with great peace and joy. Seeing tragedy as an opportunity to grow his faith and whole personhood, the author seeks to show inner healing in spite of lack of physical cure—an unadulterated triumph of spirit over circumstance. Bad situations may not be God's purpose, but Emens believes we can make them purposeful.

Emens graduated with an undergraduate degree from Kenyon College, a Master's degree from the London School of Economics, and a doctorate from Miami University. He also attended the seminary Methodist Theological School in Ohio. Most recently, he retired from The Ohio State University at the Marion campus, where he was twice voted *"Teacher of the Year"* by the student body. His previous text, **WTO Panel Dynamics**, was published in 2007, and reprinted in 2012. He lives with his wife in Marion, Ohio. He has two stepchildren and two grandchildren.

www.ingramcontent.com/pod-product-compliance
Lightning Source LLC
Chambersburg PA
CBHW060556100426
42742CB00013B/2578